Insensible Heart

Insensible Heart

by Maureen Jivani

*To Ali
love
Maureen Jivani*

Published 2009 by Mulfran Press
PO Box 812, Cardiff CF11 1PD
UK
www.mulfran.co.uk

The right of Maureen Jivani
to be identified as author of this work has been
asserted in accordance with the Copyright,
Designs and Patents Act, 1988.

Poems copyright © Maureen Jivani 2009

Cover & Stroke drawings copyright © Jill Schoenmann 2009

ISBN 978-1-907327-02-5

All rights reserved. No part of this publication may be
reproduced, stored in a retrieval system, or transmitted
at any time or by any means, electronic, mechanical,
photocopying, recording or otherwise without the prior
permission of the copyright holder, except in the case of
short extracts for inclusion in critical articles or reviews.

Printed by imprint**digital** in Devon [info@imprintdigital.net].

Acknowledgements

Thanks are due to the editors of the following publications in which these poems or versions of them have appeared or are forthcoming:

Boomslang, Magma, nthposition, Orbis, Other Poetry, Seam, Smiths Knoll, The Glasgow Review, The Frogmore Papers, The New Writer, The Rialto, THE SHOp, Trespass, The Wolf.

Grateful acknowledgements are due to all of the following for their helpful insights: Christopher Meredith and other staff and fellow students at the University of Glamorgan; Moniza Alvi and fellow students of The Poetry School; Alison Jesson, Ray Givans, Helen Overell, Catherine Strong, Rodney Wood; and special thanks to Leona Carpenter, Claire Crowther, Carrie Etter and Catherine Smith, for their close reading and comments.

for Nazim

Contents

Open Heart	11
Visiting Hours	12
Night Duty	13
Going Under	14
Sirenomyelia	15
The Pathologist's Wife	16
Portrait with Bandages	17
The Collector	18
Forensics	19
1. Ulcers	20
2. The Torturer's Day Off	21
Woman in a Bath	22
The Touring Museum of Broken Relationships	24
A Benediction in the Gallery	25
Resurrecting the Capuchin Monks	26
Priest	27
The Pathologist's Faith	28
Stone-baby	29
Pass Over	30
Apprentice Angels	31
Punch	32
Musical	33
Tunnel's End	34
Times is Hard, Mrs Lovett	35

Horse	36
Morning in the Borough of Loss	37
A Fairy Tale	38
Lessons for Cubs	39
Lessons for Bears	40
From Grandma's Bed	41
The Goldilocks Zone	42
Nursery Rhyme	43
Story	44
My Shinji Noon	46
Ghost	52
Dispatched	53
Grandmother's Treasure	54
Off Newfoundland	55
Silver	56
Stroke	57
Mind the Gap	58
In that Country	59
The Last Tobogganist	60
Harry	62
Swing	63
Trampoline	64
Yes	65
Bride	66

Open Heart

I had a heart in my hands once.
It shivered like an injured bird.
I had to stop those fibrillations
to steady that pale heart,
cooled, in its cage of bone.
Such an enormous task,
it took all the long afternoon.

But we had opera, laughter
and a tunnel of light
in that dungeon-cold room.
And sometimes it leapt,
that insensible heart, like a flying fish
or one left behind when the tide
goes out. Poor heart to be stranded
like this, a fist of blubber, in my small hands.

Visiting Hours

You're not supposed to be here.
Walking through walls – what next?

Your head tucked under your arm?
You claimed you always hated the clichéd

and snorted at doctors who afforded you
six months to live – their cock-sure words

muted by those schoolgirl nurses
who tried in vain to pat your hand;

those sainted patients bearing their crosses
with a smile and a nod; the rattle and clatter

of late-night trolleys; and hardest to bear,
the chin-up inane banter of terminal wards.

On your last trip home you spat at neighbours
who crossed the road as you were cradled
                              from the ambulance.

    Now you're back
a hopeless ghost filling the void between God
and the devil though you never believed in either.

Why not stay put beneath the soil
like any decent atheist? There's nothing here
to keep you; but look once more if you must

at your silenced wife, broken sons,
your grandkids tending snowmen.

Night Duty

In darkness, you have climbed
to the top of the stairs
to a corridor of endless doors.

Beneath your feet
the building sighs
like all the deceased
you've ever known
laid out on hospital sheets,
bodies cleansed and shrouded
             for the viewing.

You could open a door at any point,
perhaps here where the stairwell
                           twists
          and spirals.

Yet you pass by, whistling
for all the dead, telling yourself
your heart still beats, knowing
you hang on mystery.

Going Under

Here, waiters are tall and carry silver salvers:
the dead on a plate, cabinet doors open and close
of their own accord. Venetian crystal sparkles
like a new love. The hostess grins while flaming Sambucas.

                        Faces float
masks accumulating dust.
A woman breezes past
wearing gold shoes and a décolletage to die for.

In the mirror, an elderly man
removes his gloves; one slips in silence to the floor.
The grandfather clock chimes the hour.

I sigh in an effort of remembrance.

An upstairs bedroom, a drab light spools through shutters,
spills across a bedraggled bed, a white glove resting
on a bedside table.

I turn, expecting a kiss I once knew.

Sirenomyelia

Five little sweethearts, open mouthed,
in blue glass jars. He's commissioned
an artist, working in oils, to capture
their splendour, their perfect flaws.

He directs him to detail the green of eyes,
the cream of skin, the clavicles' erotic curves,
those outstretched arms, unformed breasts,
and the human scars of the umbilicus,

to pay attention below their waists
to the fusion of bones, the splayed fans
of metatarsals. Easy to see where problems lie.
Sometimes at night they hear them singing.

The Pathologist's Wife

dresses in silk, fastens his gift
of fresh-water pearls around her neck,
fingering each stone like a rosary bead.

She must compose herself before the influx
of guests. All things are done. Or will be soon.
She has removed the ice,

topped, tailed, gutted and cleaved
the oceans of flesh, and left him to soak
in a light marinade of lemons and dill.

Portrait with Bandages

The face, evident from those peep-hole eyes
of charcoal grey, those pin-point pupils
staring back. Look closer, lips
are parted as if about to tongue a kiss.

The wrap of neck, perfectly executed,
each two-inch overlap beautifully wound
by the hands of another who loved such
willingness to please – the childlike quality.

Plump breasts compressed beneath crepe
just enough to let imagination loosen
in those who come to view her framed
like this, silent and correctly bound.

The Collector

Mornings, he weeps because he loves them:
arch of aorta, cerebral cortex,
heart, lung, mammary glands…

He sets them floating in glass jars
and sits for hours to record
the intricacies of spleen and tongue.

Afternoons, he spends drawing:
a portfolio of flesh and bones
where his tears leave stiffened prints

on each turned page.
He knows he must master it all,
Abdominal to Zygote, before the end of day

when all he'll do is look so hard
his cytoplasm will set like jelly
and his eyes dry out.

Forensics

for CC

Exhibit A:

Saliva secreted on the mannequin found in a room at Eden Place – of female form the piece was arranged on a bed of nails below a lit painting of a scrappy moon.

Exhibit B:

Wolf-fur found on the largest pair of prosthetic hands, those situated around the object's throat. Hands were placed at the waist, hips, and thighs. Ankles and breasts, tightly bound with measuring tape.

Exhibit C:

Bite-marks found on a chest of drawers containing twenty-five assorted wigs, woven from straightened pubic hair – shades of blonde, red and black, varying in length and ethnic styles.

Exhibit D:

Ten fingernails (shaped into miniature hearts) found in a box of The Taylor's Chalk, in possession of the gentleman present, who, when questioned, denied the account of her absent head.

1. Ulcers

He was taught to pull wings slowly
off damselflies and watch them crawl.
His father had said, torture's an art
requiring control, but for weeks now
this son has failed to extract
one useful confession from the toothless hags.
In the Lords' chambers there is talk of reprieves.
He suspects daggers behind his back.

And there's a fire in the pit of his stomach.
His mother, tutting at the bare table,
continues to knit. Each clickety-clack
drums holes in his head.

He belches, covers the stink
with an unwashed hand.
Forgive me, he says.

What's that? she snaps.
What would your father say?
Shame on you. Shame.

2. The Torturer's Day Off

On his first free day from a month
of screams he walks to the fields
for sweeter air but crows blacken the sky,
winging to the land where year after year,
despite his work, the crops have died.

And as he thinks about how it might be
if witchcraft ceased, if he were to sleep
without dreams in the folds of a wife
instead of plundering the hearts of women
who never confess,

he sees crows dance on the shoulders
                              of straw men,

stab at their breasts,
                unpick their mouldering seams.

Woman in a Bath

> *I cry out for order and find it only in art.*
> Helen Hayes

A watchman patrolling the gallery
at night, bored with his lot,
shrugging off an exhibition

of *The Forties' Siren*, might
loosen his tie, set down
his mug, and arriving

at you, note how your right
arm shields your breasts,
permits no liberties,

might focus instead on the ash
blonde hair, the revelation
of facial bones

or how your clear eyes fix
on something unimaginable
out of shot –

the breathtaking

complexity of a room
so bluntly tiled, though vogue
for its time, the shower

taps, the three soap
dishes, a portrait of Hitler
on the edge,

the way a grey jacket
embraces a chair
or the wrist-watch drapes

like a badge of honour;
perhaps those Para boots
standing undone

on the bathroom floor
finish him off
as a stony Aphrodite

looks blankly on.

The Touring Museum of Broken Relationships

did not contain the ear of Van Gogh
but possessed a false leg, lily white,

feminine, such a pleasing thigh,
donated by a lady of the Dutch Aristocracy

together with words embroidered on silk
which when translated read,

My prosthesis has endured longer
than my love.

But of course, some words lack truth.
The leg was male, donated by a veteran

of the Bosnian war
who had one time been smitten

by a slim-hipped social-worker
who'd helped him procure it.

This is true, though not embroidered on silk.

A Benediction in the Gallery
   for CS

Naked before saints, we've held
our embrace for far too long; I'm beginning

to notice the weight of my hips. The conch
of his ear, my one point of view. A gentleman

would change position, turn a little
on the plinth. He whispers that there are others

present, perched on rocks, coupled
by muscle; a sea of still flesh, open-mouthed

sinners. Are those prayers from the faithful,
rising over his shoulders? If he cocked

his head a fraction, I might catch them
in supreme agitation of perpetual

habits, gasping at our marbled thighs,
their hands rubbing over rosaries.

Resurrecting the Capuchin Monks

After we had restored the bones,
Reconstituted organs and flesh,
Their tonsured heads, we clothed
Each one in hooded robes, danced them
Along the Dolce Vita to an all-American
Style café, served them cappuccinos
In over-sized cups, and as Brando
Peered down from his IL PADRINO
Poster we offered them a cure for pox,
Rock from the moon, cellular phones,

A few good years, in exchange
For their views on a life beyond
But tight-lipped they cowered
Low in their chairs mourning their art,
Their crypts of creation, mosaics
Of loss: skeletal brethren rearranged
By their hands: arabesques of skulls
And scapulae, knucklebone wreaths,
Ribbed chandeliers, garlanded hips,
Those winged hourglasses, butterflies.

Priest

He's moody like Brando
but this isn't a take and he's
no star perfecting lines
into existence here on Harlan's
frozen bay where he skates
alone below a deadpan sky
lips barely parted rehearsing a prayer –

a cut of wind
flings out the skirt of his cassock
like a flag at half-mast

and he clasps his hands behind
his back; one boot scarring
the carapace of ice, the other

jitters in the chill – mid-air.

The Pathologist's Faith

lies on steel.
A dead heart
weighing less than a pound.

He picks it up.
It is a map of scars,
empty vessel,

fallen crown.

He thrusts it back
inside the ribs.
Its rotten odour

clings to his gloves
as he recalls
a poetic image:

the deluded turtle's
sightless crawl
towards parched soil.

Stone-baby

Lodestone,
I hold you in my palm,
trace the outline of skull, torso, limbs.

I hold you to my ear
expecting a heartbeat
or at least the echo of a heartbeat.

Awkward fruit,
I will name you a sacred name.
I will offer you my own stopped heart.

I will bow
beneath each new moon
to sing at your altar.

Pass Over

Down Crescent Moon Lane
    over the Wey's shaky bridge

past the lilac-heavy hedge, past
    the white butterfly skirting

the hawthorn, past the cemetery
    with the churchyard billboard

Know the Meaning of Contemporary Faith

    three green balloons

    blown
            through air

quiver in a fitful wind, collide and part,
    collide and part

back and forth, east to west,
    ribbons anchored to the ash.

Apprentice Angels

balanced on vapour trails
looking neither left nor right,

concentrate on weightlessness,
empty their hearts of lovers or murderers,
of earth and sea, learn how not to fall.

Below, words echo choruses
of prayer and praise. They do not hear.

We raise our heads to passing planes,
imagine landscapes beyond our reach,

fail to see the trembling in the sky,
the uncertainty of wings.

Punch

There are stars floating beneath its froth;
he holds it to the light and squinting
finds the face of Christ all bleeding heart
and pleading eyes. He drops his drink
and staggers out from these dim pub lights
into a darker deeper night. And howls,
Oh if this universe, this God-forsaken
universe has split its skin
am I to blame? And crashed upon
the bleary ground, slurs *never again.*
        Never again.

Musical

Among parliament's debris a musician
       stands on the fractured roof
             watching crows peck themselves to rags

flies hemming their legs to the lost…
       And he fiddles for change,
             taxies, aeroplanes, untold debts.

Tunnel's End

Let's say you meet an angel
complete with wings and robe
on the tube to Tooting Broadway
who offers you a crystal glass
filled with snow and it doesn't seem strange
though this is August and the day hot.
He disappears into the crowd at Clapham South.

Perhaps then, you get off the train
and see the girl. The one you saw yesterday,
and each day before. Only this time you stop.
She doesn't ask for money or a cigarette;
she simply holds out her hands. You give her the glass.
You touch. The snow begins to melt
and it doesn't seem odd. It doesn't seem odd at all.

Times is Hard, Mrs Lovett
Sweeney Todd

The whore folds
herself into him,

her left hand
presses down

on his groin,
Such times, lover,

*brings us
closer to God.*

Horse

Word's out there's a stash in the coop
but this mare no longer chases tales
though I can sniff them lucid and living.

It probably began with chicken fever
puncturing the groin's puckered veins.
Now I'm a crock of bin laden's best.

Morning in the Borough of Loss

A woman is moving
above London, breaststroking
through air, through cloud,

over the Thames, St Paul's dome,
Canary Wharf.
On the Isle of Dogs

a child stalked by a Jaguar
breaks
        into a run.

In Ravenscourt Park
a beagle
        snaps
free of its leash,

nose to the ground,
hammers towards
        the falling bird.

And in Goldhawk Road
a woman jump-
        falls

in her sleep, wakes
to the howls of a bitch,
the grief of larks,

her flawless heart.

A Fairy Tale

Quiet in the woods.
The children sleep beneath the boughs.
See how the birds have covered them
with leaves. They are dreaming of sugar
while the witch is busy with incantations,
checking the thermostat on her new stove.

Back home there is trouble. Father is drunk.
Mother is scolding. It's a worn-out story.
The narrator grows tired. Wishes he
could change the plot. But this is hard.

Above the trees a bird flaps its wings,
comes home to roost. And in the blink
of an owl, the pages turn.

Can you hear the chiming?
Somewhere in a far-off land,
candles are lit, prayers are said.
Wait. See the children stir.
Quiet. We must hold our breath.

Lessons for Cubs

> ...*in the distant past, humans and animals were not as clearly distinguished as they are today.*
> Encyclopaedia of World Myths

Remember a skinned bear may look like man.
Never take off your coat in company.

We are not only hunters but hunted.
Wherever possible cover your tracks.

Do not be caught out at small talk, or debating.
The philosophy of consciousness is a trap.

Growls will strengthen the oppressor's axe.
Keep this in mind. Even as parading on two legs

gains us height our noses will be further
from the ground.

Lessons for Bears

She dreamt herself full grown,
a naked woman, teaching a bear in a wood
to dance. They'd begin with a waltz
and he'd nuzzle his snout in the crook of her neck
and forget all the steps. Next they'd try to tango

but he was inept, crushing her so close
to his chest she'd smell the smoke
in his ragged pelt. He'd try to whisper
but his voice was a heavy-weight of growl
thundering to the forest floor,

*I forgive you these hot coals, these iron chains
this scaling down from beast to prince
but never…*

She would wake to his idle body,
his glass-eyed stare, his useless tongue.

From Grandma's Bed

ridiculous in a frilly bonnet,
the wolf's head protrudes;
its tongue lolls from its mouth.

The bedside lamp offers no hope,
dull in its energy-efficient watt.
The wolf can barely see through her glasses;

its big eyes squint at the hands of the clock,
the bossy shadows cast on the walls;
its big ears cock at the wind's attempt

to copycat voice, like a child's cry fresh
from her lips, it makes no sense of this.
And where is grandpa all this time?

Scrubbing his britches out in the sink
in a secret room at the back of the house.
Stroking his wolf whiskers, aligning his thoughts,

consorting with poets and storytellers.
Yet who knows what trouble prowls
a wolf's mind as it shifts about in its bone

and fur, the bearded analyst out in Vienna,
the innocent walking alone in the woods,
the dreaming parents snug in their beds?

The Goldilocks Zone

They keep a window open
in case she returns, light candles
for their golden one; they named
an ecosphere after her.

She was the one they hadn't meant to scare;
the one they could have, would have loved.

She'd jammed her bedroom windows shut,
closed out planets, improbable stars.
Gouged out the eyes of her teddy bears.

Nursery Rhyme

Three children playing Hot Cross Buns on pennywhistles,
over a grave: I found this somewhere, in a poem or a story

I can't now source. No matter, the image returns time
and again, ambushes me as I go about setting the table,

poaching eggs, buttering toast, or out for a walk.
Sometimes I see the faces of those tiny musicians

in children who linger behind passing parents,
their pure notes rising to my inner ear.

Story

Once, grandmother Lyssa,
wearing red clothes
and the dog's-head cap

her ancestors made,
walked through a field of snow,
carrying her mother's basket

packed with flour and eggs
to bake a cake for her grandma.
There were jewels in the snow,

she gathered them up –
glittering icing for the cake –
and entered the woods

to the crunch of her footsteps
and the song of a jay
but as the wind started to howl

her feet would not carry her
any further, as if they knew
her grandma had flown,

her parents were calling,
that the wolf waiting beneath
the crocheted shawl

was her whiskered self.
Snow blanked out her world;
cold fingered her bones.

When the doctor arrived,
in his long coat and gloves,

she was brittle as twigs,

stiffened as bark,

                snapped,

I've forgotten my age

though I know how my story ends
with grandwolves and mad dogs
in the white-haired wood.

My Shinji Noon

> *Things are not what they seem;*
> *Nor are they otherwise.* –
> Lankavatara Sutra

1. Notes from a Concubine

the tiny worm spins silk from its mouth

the works of men should match the works of heaven

water   rock   pavilion   plants

my Shinji Noon   half-man   half-bird

flint   wood   fire

China is middle Earth   Emperor is China

lion head   serpent body

flowering houses   opium dens

feather and scale   nest side by side

our Emperor's tongue speaks in gold

our silks are forbidden to fade

2. Flight

Some nights when emperor's bed
excited by others I go to room
of imperial artist   watch him breed
life for phoenix on imperial silk

later   sip orange blossom tea
in shadow of moon   slip down robe
attend rhythm of caged heartbeat
stroke wings   unfold to hold up sky

3. The Imperial Artist Shinji Noon

paints humbled tigers
tumbling through hoops

ladies with fans
bows   bound feet

pagodas of gold
gold flags flying

other times
my Shinji Noon

is bad tempered chi
belly-full of devils

tells me Buddha
sits scratching His head

while our parents'
daughters are hoofed

into dust   perhaps
he paint this?

my Shinji Noon,
on length of silk

luscious and fine
as palace walls

4. Eunuch

Shinji Noon
sleeps

beneath
cypress

late afternoon
sun fierce

like dragons' eyes
Shinji Noon

dreams

hunch down tiger
in far away jungle

circle him slowly

round and round

go hunch down tiger
until flop

on jungle floor
and roll

expose rounded
belly

each tooth
in Shinji Noon's

mouth uproot
fall to ground

dream finish
Shinji Noon

wake to cypress
unwavering shield

5. The Emperor's Monkey

Night of conception
imperial monkey
escape from cage
of emperor's room

nails claw silk
of imperial artist
tooth and fur
shiver to frenzy

monkey beautiful
blue face   coat
orange flame
why monkey mad?

live imperial
no need to forage
forest or mountain
home here   sea of jade

6. Shinji Noon Grows Thin

Orange blossom tea

not help restore

my Shinji Noon
diminish beneath robes

healer he leave potion
crush dragon   tiger bone

seven seahorse
aroma of yang

I rub imperial artist limb
press ear to chest

listen   wind chimes
             broken glass

       where is heart
my Shinji Noon?

follow eyes
     to highest window

black night cold stars

Ghost

Once he was flying
              chasing her up
                          and down
                                    the stairs
              with his shirt unbuttoned
                          his arms out-stretched.

Now he's static
in an unlit corner
of the top-floor landing
and only the bangs
        of dark birds
             against the window

make her jump,
leave her stunned.

Dispatched

Here in this airless space before the church
where trees are waving beyond the graves,

I am trying to explain my final absence
from those rasping days before you left.

Children drift by, wearing your blue eyes,
handing me flowers.

Grandmother's Treasure

Beneath her bed,
buried in a box,
wrapped in tissue-paper:
amber silk, diamante
buckles, the smell
of unworn soles.
Her dancing shoes, size 4.

Off Newfoundland

A sequinned
dance shoe
lies on its side
by a crate
of champagne
and three pearl
hair combs
spike the seabed
while a murky
hand mirror
reflects
on nothing
as a drift
of ghosts
lost on their way
to the ballroom
turn to the music
of a string
band playing.

Silver

*when a man is capable of being in uncertainties, mysteries,
doubts, without any irritable reaching after fact and reason –*
Keats

In the red and gold lounge of The Hotel Marriott
I am struggling with Keats, and the meaning
of *Negative Capability*, when I overhear,
from the middle-aged couple a few seats away,
*No, not Mothers' Day. We can't have our wedding celebration
on Mothers' Day.* I want to ask why, but this is inappropriate
and I realise it the moment the waitress sets down the teapot,
the china cup and saucer, and the little tray of fancies
I'd ordered as I'd thought of the consumptive poet.
And now the tapestries of curtains are framing a slow fall
of leaves, soft autumnal light, and the silver of clouds
which the wind begins to roll like days, months, years, into one.

Stroke

In this language there will always be mothers
voiced in silk, floating like songs over a crib;

mothers invariably found on a swing or lodged
in a tree, pockets full of marbles, apples or worms;

there will always be mothers home from the march,
lit by fire, animated behind the Morning Star;

mothers arriving from Outer Mongolia, or Timbuktu,
handing round trophies of hand-painted gifts.

But heavens, don't think I know all this
by accident or that there isn't any more left to ask.

Do stars wonder at what we are?
Does the moon absorb us with its effaceable grin?

The answers are dissolving on your mother-tongue
but our days are alive and singing.

Mind the Gap

Look. Here are things we've yet to speak of,
a woman in Chinese silk, her strange shoes,

how we examine footwear, ankles, knees,
        avert our eyes,

or the day I managed to study her thigh
from station to station,

measuring the distance in undetectable sighs,

then there's this clutching of baggage
and mobile phones which fail to connect

when we need them.

In that Country

You did not kiss me
in a hotel room,

one with blistering paintwork
and an over-night ensemble

laid out on a single bed.
Nor did we talk about this later

in a conference room
between the keynote speaker's

brave attempt at 'The Trouble with Words'
and the delegates' response.

At coffee, we never lingered
over those last half-inches in our cups,

nor noticed the changing rhythms
in our breath, the finger-tips of space

between our hands. So at the close,
we did not dawdle in the court-yard,

fumbling for car keys, our heads spinning.
And you did not say, 'I'll miss you'

while a west wind skittered the gravel
at our feet and the green-eyed stray

wailed its lament
by the white-washed wall.

The Last Tobogganist

While others coast
down the slope
at the speed of laughter,
their scarves a backwards
salute to the ghostly air,
I consider whether

to release the brakes,
and lose control,
flip over the edge
and free-fall
to a frozen depth,
tumbling until snow
would pack my nose
and mouth, striking,
perhaps, my head
on a rock so the last
fine thing for me
to gaze on would be
this night's cold stars,

or else continue
at this solitary pace,
so slow those others
would be warming their toes
by their chalet firesides,
sipping hot chocolate
and joking
about the woman
they'd left behind
on the mountain,
at the base of a fir,
splayed like snow angels
children make.

But who might imagine me
wearing my crown of ice
like a queen, this New Year's frost
a splinter of wonder along my brow?

Harry

I want to talk about Harry,

the way he makes me laugh,
his obsessions with Scotland,
anatomy, espionage, how more than once
we have caught him *looking for clues*
on the official web-site of the CIA
or how his ideal trip might involve
catching a train to Glasgow
and a day at the local infirmary
to watch the dissections of blank-faced cadavers,
where he'd gleefully name those organs,
muscles and sinew piled on a trolley,
how excited he'd get on the tips of his toes,
the flap of his butterfly hands.

I want to talk about Harry.
It's hard to explain.

Swing

Dear Odin,

This image you send,
fleeting, uninvited, while I sit
combing my golden hair –

the grey rat
dead in the road,
its one accusing eye –

the spilled guts,
hard-edged paws
wasting away –

perhaps I should try
to remember myself
at four or five, high on a swing –

wind through my hair.
But what is this thing
that gnaws

at my poor heart,
claws under my skin?
Dear God –

must I really house this thing
under your false roof?
Lock it away?

What might it prove?
What might it say?

Trampoline

To bounce   in slow motion
     to fall
        in
            love
with the give
    of your knees
          to consider   the precise
    angle
      of
        toes
     to disregard   the crowds
            beneath
                    your feet
to look beyond
  those critical heads
      towards a stretch
            of blue
    cloudless and still
        as its own reflection
  in that oblivious pond
      near the sycamore.

Yes
for Lottie

You, love, behind me, arms around my waist,
our breath milking the air, the clear white slopes
of Morzine against the dark sky, and stars hung out
like lanterns for nocturnal skiers, who are descending
like angels with their gorgeous flames held high,
and most of all this child here in the crowd beside us,
whispering, *Daddy, I think I've got the winter in my ear.*

Bride

My sisters dance with grey men
in strange suits on a foreign shore.
They are learning to be quiet,
to move without music.

The wind blowing in
doesn't trouble their hair
yet stiffens their step.

While I, unobserved,
choose the rush of my skirt
dancing me into the sea.